THIS BOOK BELONGS TO

_____

_____

Books By Max

Books By Max

Books By Max

Books By Max

Books By Max

Books By Max

Books By Max

Books By Max

Books By Max

Books By Max

Books By Max

Books By Max

Books By Max

Books By Max

Books By Max

Books By Max

Books By Max

Books By Max

Books By Max

Belong to

COLOR TEST PAGE

Made in the USA
Las Vegas, NV
19 December 2024

14768472R00057